ELECTRICITY

ELECTRICITY

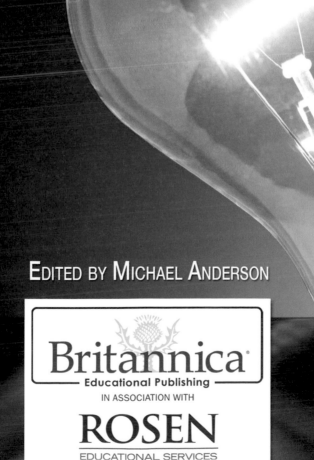

EDITED BY MICHAEL ANDERSON

Britannica
Educational Publishing

IN ASSOCIATION WITH

ROSEN
EDUCATIONAL SERVICES

Published in 2012 by Britannica Educational Publishing
(a trademark of Encyclopædia Britannica, Inc.)
in association with Rosen Educational Services, LLC
29 East 21st Street, New York, NY 10010.

Distributed exclusively by Rosen Educational Services.
For a listing of additional Britannica Educational Publishing titles, call toll free (800) 237-9932.

First Edition

Britannica Educational Publishing
Michael I. Levy: Executive Editor, Encyclopædia Britannica
J.E. Luebering: Director, Core Reference Group, Encyclopædia Britannica
Adam Augustyn: Assistant Manager, Encyclopædia Britannica

Anthony L. Green: Editor, Compton's by Britannica
Michael Anderson: Senior Editor, Compton's by Britannica
Andrea R. Field: Senior Editor, Compton's by Britannica
Sherman Hollar: Associate Editor, Compton's by Britannica

Marilyn L. Barton: Senior Coordinator, Production Control
Steven Bosco: Director, Editorial Technologies
Lisa S. Braucher: Senior Producer and Data Editor
Yvette Charboneau: Senior Copy Editor
Kathy Nakamura: Manager, Media Acquisition

Rosen Educational Services
Hope Lourie Killcoyne: Senior Editor and Project Manager
Nelson Sá: Art Director
Cindy Reiman: Photography Manager
Karen Huang: Photo Researcher
Matthew Cauli: Designer, Cover Design
Introduction by Hope Lourie Killcoyne

Library of Congress Cataloging-in-Publication Data

Electricity / edited by Michael Anderson.—1st ed.
    p. cm.—(Introduction to physics)
"In association with Britannica Educational Publishing, Rosen Educational Services."
Includes bibliographical references and index.
ISBN 978-1-61530-665-7 (library binding)
1. Electricity—Juvenile literature. I. Anderson, Michael, 1972–
QC527.2.E44 2012
537—dc23

                                                                    2011017090

Manufactured in the United States of America

On the cover, page 3: An electric current flows through the wires and filament of this tungsten light
bulb and allows it to burn bright. *Shutterstock.com*

Cover (equation), interior background images Shutterstock.com

CONTENTS

Electricity is a form of energy whose discovery led to a fundamental change in human life and civilization as we know it. Without it, we would have no computers or cable boxes, no microwaves or motorcycles, no refrigerators or radios, no telephones or toasters. There would be no lights, no cameras, and no action.

That's right: no action. Because while we may think of electricity as happening *outside* our bodies—from the lightning that crackles across the sky to the lights we turn on with the flip of a switch—our bodies *themselves* (including that very index finger doing the switch flicking) host a plethora of electric signals all the time. (Shocking but true.)

The essential thing to know about electricity—and the reason it occurs both naturally and as a result of our having learned to harness or generate it—is that the big players involved are actually microscopically tiny particles—atoms, which are, of course, everywhere. But it goes even deeper, because the real stars of the electricity show are even smaller than the atom. What ultimately results in the energy we call electricity comes down to movement of the smallest order *within* the atom. That is, movement of each atom's principal tenants: a proton (which has a positive electrical charge) and an electron (which has a negative charge). Positive and negative charges, which are attracted to each other, try to move close together. Conversely, two like charges (whether both positive or both negative) push each other away. All that pushing and pulling results in electricity.

How can we come to understand this omnipresent power? Again, here are two fundamental things to remember about electricity:

1. It occurs naturally, as in that bolt of lightning or the beat of your heart. (It is, in fact, the heart's ability to conduct electricity that keeps the blood pumping.)
2. Electricity can also be generated, as at power plants. From there, it is sent through wires to your home where it powers the television, the lights, and anything else that plugs in. It can also be stored, as in the batteries inside a laptop computer, a Nintendo DS, or a cell phone.

One of electricity's brightest ideas, the lightbulb, has long represented the initial spark of human thought and creativity. © www.istock-photo.com/ Bart Coenders

This book offers a concise view of electricity—its history and how it works. Readers will discover just what causes the

sometimes hair-raising power of static electricity, as well as how electric fields work. These pages also explore and explain what happens when electricity flows, the relationship between electricity and magnetism, how motors and generators fit into the electromagnetic landscape, and how centuries of discoveries (both accidental and intentional) have changed our understanding of and ability to control electricity. It is worth noting, and is probably no accident, that the visual metaphor for that most central of all human creations—the idea—is expressed by a lightbulb.

Although electricity is a form of power that has transformed everyday life, it nonetheless often takes a power outage for us to consider just how important electricity is to everything that we do. This book shows just what is behind the awesome power of those impossibly tiny particles—the electron and the proton—and how their movement is essential to life itself.

CHAPTER 1

THE FUNDAMENTALS OF ELECTRICITY

Electricity is a form of energy associated with the atomic particles called electrons and protons. In particular, electricity involves the movement or accumulation of negatively charged electrons in relation to positively charged protons. The world's modern economies, with their industrial, transportation, and communication systems, were made possible by electricity. Old energy forms, such as water and steam, imposed limitations on production—limitations on where goods could be produced and on how much could be produced. Electricity has few such limits: it can go anywhere, even far into space.

The development of electricity has resulted in the total transformation of civilization. It brings power into homes to operate lights, kitchen appliances, television sets, radios, furnaces, computers, garage doors,

and more. So common are its uses that one cannot imagine today's world without it. Streets would not be lit. Telephones would not work. Storefronts and factories would be dimmed.

Electrical forces are also responsible for holding body cells together in the shape they have. In fact, electrical forces are fundamental in holding all matter together. As printed words are being read, electric currents speed along nerve cells from eye to brain. The effect of an electric current can be seen in the flash of lightning between thundercloud and Earth as well as in the spark that can be produced when one walks on a carpet in a dry room.

STATIC ELECTRICITY AND ELECTRIC CHARGE

Understanding electricity begins with describing its effects. One way to begin is to examine interactions that occur when electricity is at rest, in a form called static electricity. Static electricity can be seen at work when hair is combed on a cold, dry day. As the comb is pulled through, strands of hair stand out stiffly. Some kind of force

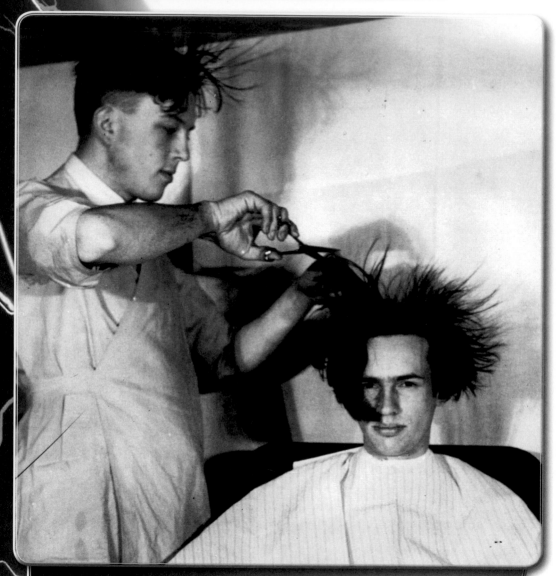

This barber employs the novel technique of cutting a customer's hair after it has been charged with static current, making it stand on end and thus, presumably, easier to cut. **General Photographic Agency/ Hulton Archive/Getty Images**

seems to pull the strands upward toward the comb. To understand the nature of this force it is necessary to know something about the concept of electric charge and the structure of atoms.

Simple experiments can illustrate how electric charge works. If a glass rod is rubbed with silk and touched to a small sphere of aluminum foil suspended by a thread, the sphere moves away from the glass rod. The rod and sphere repel each other. If the process is repeated with a second sphere and the spheres are brought near each other, they too repel. If a plastic rod is rubbed with wool and brought near either sphere, the spheres move toward the plastic rod. These objects attract each other. If two new aluminum foil spheres are touched to the plastic rod, they are repelled by the plastic, as well as by each other. But they are attracted to the glass rod and the spheres touched by the glass rod.

These experiments can be explained by a two-charge model. Rubbing the glass with silk causes the glass to acquire a positive charge. When touched to the spheres it shares some of its positive charge with the spheres and these objects repel. Rubbing the plastic with

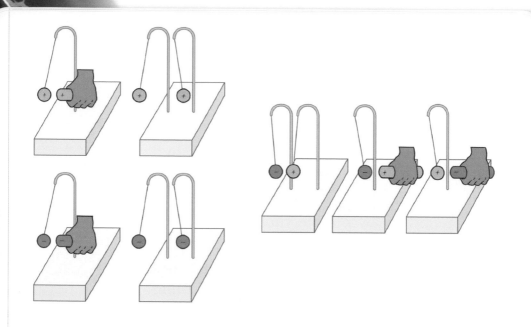

Aluminum foil spheres (blue) are touched by a glass rod (blue) that has been rubbed with silk. These have positive charges and repel each other. Other aluminum foil spheres (orange) are touched by a plastic rod (orange) that has been rubbed with wool. These have negative charges and repel each other. Spheres with like charges also repel each other. Oppositely charged spheres and rods, however, attract each other. **Copyright Encyclopædia Britannica, Inc.; rendering for this edition by Rosen Educational Services**

wool causes the plastic to acquire a negative charge. When touched to the spheres it shares some of its negative charge with the spheres and these objects repel.

This interpretation of the experiment leads to the conclusion that like charges repel. But when a positively charged sphere is brought near a negatively charged plastic rod or sphere, the objects attract each other. And when a negatively charged sphere is brought near a positively charged glass rod, the objects attract each other. This leads to the conclusion that unlike charges attract. No matter how an object is charged, if it attracts the negatively charged sphere, it will also repel the positively charged sphere, and vice versa. This leads to the belief that there are only two kinds of electric charge.

ELECTRIC CHARGES IN ATOMS

A model of matter is needed to explain how only two kinds of charged rods can be produced. Atoms contain two kinds of charge, which are arbitrarily called positive and negative. Every atom is composed of a positively charged nucleus around which are distributed negatively charged electrons. Each nucleus contains a specific number of protons—particles that carry the positive charge. (With the exception of the hydrogen atom, nuclei also contain uncharged

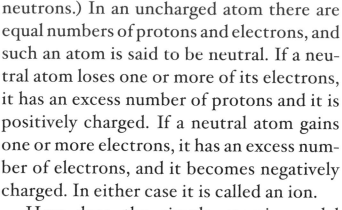

neutrons.) In an uncharged atom there are equal numbers of protons and electrons, and such an atom is said to be neutral. If a neutral atom loses one or more of its electrons, it has an excess number of protons and it is positively charged. If a neutral atom gains one or more electrons, it has an excess number of electrons, and it becomes negatively charged. In either case it is called an ion.

How does the simple atomic model relate to the static electricity experiments? Rubbing action creates charged objects because it tears electrons loose from some kinds of atoms and transfers them to others. In the case of plastic rubbed with wool, electrons are taken from the wool and pile up on the plastic, giving the plastic a net negative charge and leaving the wool charged positively. When glass is rubbed with silk, the glass loses electrons and the silk gains electrons, making the glass positively charged and the silk negatively charged.

THE EFFECT OF DISTANCE ON ELECTRIC FORCE

In the 18th century French physicist Charles-Augustin de Coulomb (after whom the basic unit of electric charge is named) showed the

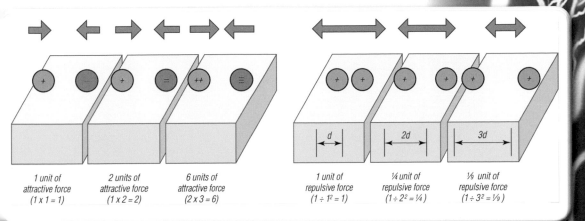

| 1 unit of attractive force (1 x 1 = 1) | 2 units of attractive force (1 x 2 = 2) | 6 units of attractive force (2 x 3 = 6) | 1 unit of repulsive force (1 ÷ 1² = 1) | ¼ unit of repulsive force (1 ÷ 2² = ¼) | ⅑ unit of repulsive force (1 ÷ 3² = ⅑) |

The amount of electrostatic force between two charges is directly proportional to the product of the charges (left) and inversely proportional to the square of the distance between the charges (right). **Encyclopædia Britannica, Inc.**

relationship between the strength of the electric force that two charged objects exert upon each other and the distance separating them. For two point charges (a point charge is a charged sphere whose radius is very small compared to its distance from a second point charge), carrying charges q_1 and q_2, whose centers are separated by distance d, the electric force F is determined by:

$$F = \frac{k q_1 q_2}{d^2}$$

In this equation, k is a constant, meaning that it is generally assumed to have the same value

French physicist Charles-Augustin de Coulomb (left) *and English physicist and mathematician Sir Isaac Newton* (right). *Two central terms in the vocabulary of electricity—the coulomb and the newton—are named after them.* **SSPL via Getty Images (left), Time & Life Pictures/Getty Images (right).**

at all places and at all times. If the charges are measured in coulombs (*C*) and the distance in meters (*m*), the electric force can be calculated in newtons (*N*) with the conversion constant:

$$k = 9.0 \times 10^9 \ N \, m^2/C^2$$

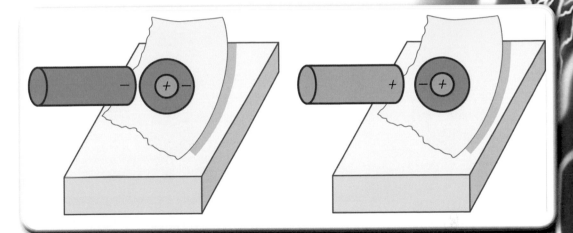

One atom is attracted by a negatively charged rod (left) *and by a positively charged rod* (right). Copyright Encyclopædia Britannica, Inc.; rendering for this edition by Rosen Educational Services

ELECTROSTATIC INDUCTION

The fact that electrical force decreases rapidly as the distance between the charges increases is important in explaining another observation about static electricity. If a charged rod (whether positive or negative) is brought near some uncharged bits of paper, the paper is initially attracted to the rod. How can this happen? When a positively charged rod is brought near a neutral scrap of paper, the electrons in each atom of the paper are drawn somewhat toward the rod and the nuclei, which are positive, are pushed slightly

COMMON EXAMPLES OF ELECTROSTATIC INDUCTION

The principle of electrostatic induction can be seen at work in industry and in nature. Electrostatic air cleaners attract neutral dust particles to a charged screen by induction. The electrostatic scrubbers used to clean the smoke produced by coal-burning power plants use the same principle on a larger scale. Charging by induction also occurs when the lower, negatively charged regions of thunderclouds induce a positive charge on Earth's surface. If the charges become large enough, the resistance of the air is overcome and lightning occurs.

away. This repositioning of the charges in the neutral scrap of paper is called electrostatic induction.

Because the electrons on the average will be slightly closer to the positive rod than to the nuclei, the force of attraction will be somewhat larger than the force of repulsion. Thus the paper experiences a net attractive force, and it is drawn toward the rod. A negatively charged rod will also attract uncharged bits of paper, but the repositioning of charges in the paper is reversed. Again, the attractive force will be somewhat larger than the repelling force.

CHAPTER 2

ELECTRIC FIELDS

Charged objects can exert forces on uncharged objects over a distance. The electric field provides a way to describe the effect of the electric force at

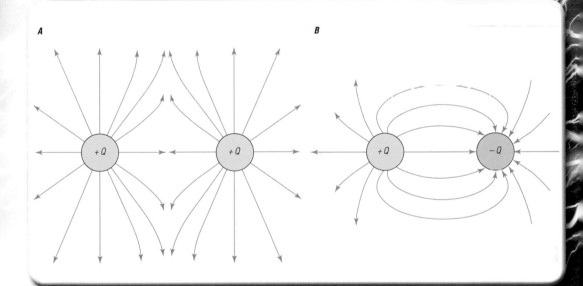

A   B

Lines of force between two similarly charged point charges veer away from each other (A). Lines of force between oppositely charged point charges merge toward each other (B). Encyclopædia Britannica, Inc.

points in space around an electric charge. The electric field strength at a point, E, is defined as the ratio of the electric force F on a test charge to the size of the test charge, q_{test}, placed at that point:

$$E = F/q_{test}$$

(A test charge is an infinitesimal charge placed in an electric field to probe the strength of the field.) This formula defines a specific value for E at each point in space. Regardless of the size of the test charge, the ratio of electric force to q_{test} will be a particular value at each position in the field.

STRENGTH

The strength of an electric field is a vector quantity. Vectors have direction as well as magnitude. An arrow can be used to represent the electric field strength: the stronger the field, the longer the arrow. The direction of the electric field vector is taken to be the same as the direction of the electric force on a positive test charge placed in the field. If the separate electric field vectors for many points in space are joined, lines

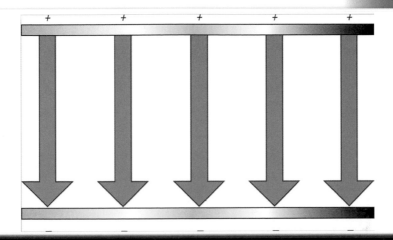

The lines of force, which are represented by arrows, are parallel in a uniform electric field between two oppositely charged plates. Copyright Encyclopædia Britannica, Inc.; rendering for this edition by Rosen Educational Services

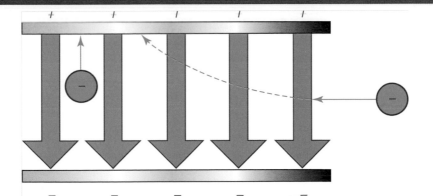

An electron (left) accelerates uniformly toward the positive plate in a uniform electric field. A horizontally moving electron (right) follows a parabolic path in the field. *Copyright Encyclopædia Britannica, Inc.; rendering for this edition by Rosen Educational Services*

are obtained that give an overview of the electric field. These lines, called lines of force, were conceived by the 19th-century English scientist Michael Faraday. Where these lines are more concentrated, the field is stronger and the electric force on a test charge will be larger. If a positive test charge is placed somewhere in the field, the force on that charge will be directed along a line tangent to the field line.

UNIFORM ELECTRIC FIELDS

An especially simple electric field occurs in the space between two oppositely charged flat plates. The field lines are equally spaced between the plates, showing that the electric field strength is the same everywhere. Such a field is called a uniform electric field. An electron placed in such a field at any spot in the field will accelerate at a constant rate toward the positive plate because the electrical force on it is constant. (It should be noted that the electron, which is negatively charged, moves in a direction opposite to that of the field lines.) If an electron enters a uniform field parallel to the plates, it will veer toward the positive plate. The stronger the field is, the more the deflection.

Michael Faraday with some of his equipment, c. 1860. **Hulton Archive/Getty Images**

POTENTIAL DIFFERENCE

A positive test charge placed near a fixed positive point charge will accelerate away, increasing in velocity and kinetic energy. Conversely, to move this positive test charge back toward the fixed positive charge, work must be done on the test charge. The energy put into this process is stored as electric potential energy by virtue of the new position of the test charge in the field. Electric potential difference is a measure of this change in energy as the charge moves from one place to another in an electric field. Mathematically it is given by:

$$\text{electric potential difference} = \frac{\text{energy change}}{\text{charge moved}}$$

The unit for measuring electric potential difference is the volt, which is a joule of energy for every coulomb of charge. Sometimes the electric potential difference is called voltage. When there is no difference in electrical potential—that is, when there is zero voltage—between points in a field, there is no tendency for electric charge to move between those points. On the other

Nineteenth-century English physicist James Joule, for whom the unit of energy is named. Portrait painted by the artist John Collier, c. 1880. **Rischgitz/Hulton Archive/Getty Images**

hand, if there is a large potential difference between two points in a field, positive elcctric charge will tend to move from higher to lower potential; negative charge would move the opposite way.

MOVING CHARGES IN ELECTRIC FIELDS

An electrochemical cell, or battery, provides a familiar example to illustrate the movement of charges in an electric field. A dry cell battery rated at 1.5 volts has an electric potential at the positive terminal that is 1.5 volts above that of the negative. Frequently this potential difference is called the emf, or electromotive force, of the battery, but this name is misleading because the electric potential difference is not really a force; the 1.5-volt rating indicates the energy change per coulomb of electric charge moved between the terminals. Each coulomb of charge moved between the terminals acquires 1.5 joules of energy.

When connected by a conductor—a material that does not inhibit the motion of electrons—electrons move away from the negative terminal (–) toward the positive terminal (+) through the conductor.

An electromagnet made from a 1.5-volt dry cell battery, an iron nail, and some wire. Henry Groskinsky/Time & Life Pictures/ Getty Images

The electrons move in response to the electric field set up in the conductor. When the terminals of the battery are connected by an insulator—a material in which electron motion is inhibited—the electrons in the insulating medium are not moved very much. Because air is an insulator, electric charge does not move between the terminals of the dry cell until they are connected by a conductor.

If the potential difference is very high, electric charge may be moved through the field even without a good conductor. In the picture tube of a traditional television set, for example, electrons ejected from a heated electrode, called the cathode, are accelerated by a very high voltage (10,000 to 50,000 volts) and fly through an evacuated tube, crashing into a screen coated with a fluorescent material to produce the bursts of light that are seen as the picture. Such a tube is known as a cathode-ray tube, or CRT. (Moving electrons can be called "cathode rays.") Cathode-ray tubes have many other applications—for

A 16-inch (41-centimeter) circular cathode-ray television, c. 1950. The earliest cathode-ray tube TV sets had circular faces on which a rectangular picture appeared. **SSPL via Getty Images**

example, in the oscilloscopes used by medical personnel for displaying heartbeat and brain-wave data.

A SIMPLE BATTERY

A simple battery can be made from strips of zinc (Zn) and copper (Cu) metal suspended in a salt solution, which is a conductor. Prior to connecting the strips by a conductor, a dynamic equilibrium exists at each metal surface. Some zinc atoms lose a pair of electrons, becoming Zn^{2+} ions. The electrons remain on the zinc metal, while the Zn^{2+} moves into the solution. The reverse process occurs at an equal rate: Zn^{2+} ions gain two electrons and adhere to the zinc strip as zinc atoms. A similar equilibrium exists at the copper surface, involving copper metal and Cu^{2+} ions.

When the metals are connected by a conductor, these equilibria are thrown out of balance. Because zinc atoms lose electrons easier than copper atoms do, electrons are forced through the conductor from the zinc strip to the copper strip. As electrons leave the zinc, net formation of Zn^{2+} ions occurs at the zinc strip. At the copper strip, Cu^{2+} ions gain electrons, becoming copper metal. As electrons move between the zinc and

copper strips through a wire outside the cell, positive ions in the solution migrate away from the zinc strip, and negative ions move away from the copper strip. This keeps the current, or flow of charges, going.

Batteries can be constructed using a variety of chemicals. Any two substances with different affinities for electrons can be suspended in a medium that allows ions to migrate, producing a battery.

CHAPTER 3

ELECTRIC CURRENT AND CIRCUITS

The concepts of current and circuits are central to the understanding of electricity. Electric current is a flow of electric charges. The charges may be electrons, protons, ions, or even positive "holes" (absences of electrons that may be thought of as positive particles). A circuit is a path through which electric current is transmitted.

ELECTRIC CHARGES IN A CURRENT

A current can be described as either direct or alternating based on the way that charges move within it. In direct current (DC), the charges always move in the same direction through the device receiving power. Batteries and fuel cells (devices that convert the chemical energy of a fuel directly into electricity) produce direct current. In alternating current (AC), the charges move back and forth in the

device and in the wires connected to it. For many purposes either type of current is suitable, but alternating current is customarily used because it can be generated and distributed with greater efficiency. The power sent out by power plants is alternating current.

When the charge q is measured in coulombs and the time t in seconds, the current I will be expressed in amperes, which is defined as coulombs per second:

$$I = q/t$$

A one-ampere current means that one coulomb of electric charge passes each point in the circuit each second. Because each electron carries only 1.6×10^{-19} (1.6 10-quintillionths, or 1.6/10,000,000,000,000,000,000) coulomb of charge, the one-ampere current—normally used in the operation of a 120-watt incandescent bulb—implies that in one second about 6×10^{18} (6 quintillion, or 6,000,000,000,000,000,000) electrons pass each point in the filament of the bulb.

Traditionally, the direction of electric current has been described as the direction of positive charge motion (conventional current), even though in most circuits it is the

An incandescent lightbulb with filaments aglow. **Shutterstock.com**

electrons that actually move (in the opposite direction). Even though electric charge moves through the filament of the bulb, the filament itself is not charged. The amounts of positive and negative charge in the filament are equal. The positive and negative charges are simply moving in opposite directions relative to each other.

It is mainly the quantity of electric current, or the amperage—not the potential difference, or voltage—that can produce a lethal shock (though higher voltages generally cause higher currents). Currents of less than 0.005 ampere that pass through the heart are not likely to cause damage. Currents of about 0.1 ampere are usually fatal, even if endured for only one second.

CONDUCTIVITY AND RESISTANCE IN A CIRCUIT

A circuit is produced when the terminals of a battery are connected with a conductor. As described in chapter 2, chemical reactions within the battery create a potential difference between the terminals, and electrons flow in the conductor in one direction, away from the negative terminal toward the positive.

The 19th-century German physicist Georg Simon Ohm showed that the current in such a circuit was directly related to the voltage of the battery but noted that the amount of current also depended on the nature of the conductor. Different kinds of conductors differed in the degree to which

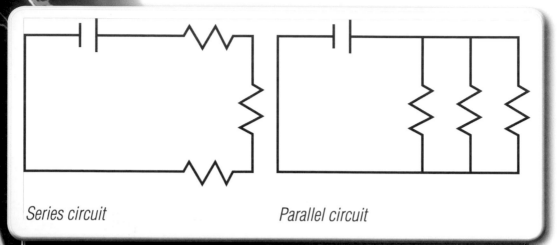

Series circuit   Parallel circuit

The symbol of two vertical lines (near the top left of each circuit) indicates a source of potential difference such as a battery. Electrons move in the circuit from the negative terminal (shorter line) toward the positive terminal (longer line). The symbol of the wavy line represents a resistor. Copyright Encyclopædia Britannica, Inc.; rendering for this edition by Rosen Educational Services

they resisted movement of electrons with a given voltage. He defined the resistance of a conductor as the ratio of the potential difference across the conductor (in volts) to the current (in amperes) through the conductor:

$$\text{resistance} = \frac{\text{potential difference}}{\text{current}} = \frac{\text{volts}}{\text{amperes}}$$

The unit of resistance is now known as the ohm, usually abbreviated as the Greek letter omega—Ω.

Georg Simon Ohm. **Hulton Archive/Getty Images**

The greater the potential difference across a circuit, the more electric current is made to flow through it and the greater the heat effects produced as electrons force their way through the wire. A wire in which a current generates a substantial quantity of heat energy is called a resistor. In a circuit diagram resistors are represented by the symbol ∧∧∧. For example, in the filament of an incandescent lightbulb and in the heating element of an electric toaster or clothes dryer, heat energy is generated as electrons are forced through these resistors. If the current is large enough, the heat generated can be used for welding metals or for smelting in electric furnaces. Two or more resistors can be connected in a circuit in series or, more often, in parallel (see section on parallel circuits).

A thicker wire offers less resistance to current than a thinner one of the same material. This is because current consists of electrons flowing through the metal of the wire. The electrons jump from atom to atom in the metal in response to the electric field in the circuit. A conductor with a larger cross section allows more electrons to interact with the field. Because there is more current with a given voltage, a conductor with a larger cross section has lower resistance.

Under special conditions, materials become superconductive, meaning all resistance disappears because electrons pair up and do not collide; current flows without losing power. Some conductors must be cooled to temperatures near -273 °C, or absolute zero, before they become superconductive. Because of the high cost of cooling such superconductors, progress in the commercial application of superconductivity was impeded. In the 1980s, however, a new class of higher-temperature superconductor was discovered. These materials are rather brittle and are difficult to form into wire, but progress is being made.

SERIES CIRCUITS

When resistors are connected in series, the electric current that flows through one resistor will flow through the next resistor and so on. Everywhere in a series circuit the current is the same. The total resistance in such a circuit is simply the sum of the resistances of the separate resistors—R_1, R_2, and so on:

$$R_{total} = R_1 + R_2 + \cdots + R_n$$

If the total potential difference across these resistors is V_t, then the current in the circuit

SWITCHES

If a circuit is complete, electrons will flow as long as the cell acts. Usually it is desirable to be able to turn current on and off. This can be done with switches, which act like a drawbridge. If the bridge is open, traffic cannot move along the road. When the bridge is closed, traffic can move. If the switch is open, current cannot flow. Closing the switch makes it possible for the current to flow. Circuits are called open or closed according to the position of the switch.

will be limited by the total resistance:

$$I_{total} = \frac{V_t}{R_1 + R_2 + \cdots + R_n}$$

The voltage drop across any particular resistor is given by:

$$V_n = I R_n$$

Wiring in series is satisfactory if the devices need only low amounts of power for operation since each added resistor will cause the current in the circuit to drop. However, if one element of the circuit burns out, the entire circuit is broken.

PARALLEL CIRCUITS

Parallel wiring allows the electric current to move through different pathways. Each

branch can be switched on or off independently, allowing some or all of the devices to
be used. In general, if the resistance along a
given parallel branch is increased, a smaller
amount of current will flow through that
branch. The more branches that are available
in parallel wiring, however, the lower the total
resistance in the circuit becomes, and thus
the higher the total current. This may seem
to be a contradiction, but it is very similar to
what happens when people leave a crowded
theater that has several exits. Although there
is resistance to movement at each exit, there
will be a larger overall rate of movement with
more exits. The total resistance for resistors
connected in parallel is given by the equation:

$$\frac{1}{R_{total}} = \frac{1}{R_1} + \frac{1}{R_2} + \ldots \frac{1}{R_n}$$

The total current that flows into the
branches will equal the sum of the currents
in each branch:

$$I_{total} = I_1 + I_2 + \ldots I_n$$

Regardless of which branch the charges fol-
low, they all move between points of equal
potential as they move through the parallel
resistors. Thus the voltages across each resistor wired in parallel are equal:

43

A power strip allows for multiple devices to be plugged in, but an overloaded strip can be a fire hazard. **Shutterstock.com**

$$V_1 = V_2 = V_n$$

Besides the advantage of being able to use resistors along each branch independently, the parallel scheme of wiring allows the addition of extra branches without changing the current in the branches already in use, thus keeping the energy consumption in each branch unchanged. In the home each

additional device that is plugged into a given circuit adds another parallel branch. But with each device added, the total resistance drops and the total current increases. If too much current flows through the conducting wires, they may overheat and a fire may occur. A fuse or a circuit breaker can be included in a parallel circuit to prevent overheating. If the current increases to a dangerous point, a filament in the fuse overheats, burns out, and the circuit is broken. In order for the parallel circuit not to be overloaded, it is necessary to remove one or more of the branches to increase the overall resistance and decrease the current.

CHAPTER 4

MAGNETIC FIELDS

Like electricity, magnetism is a fundamental force. Magnetism and electricity are closely related and are regarded as two expressions of a single force, the electromagnetic force. The region around a magnet in which magnetic forces can be seen is called a magnetic field. An electric current also creates a magnetic field.

HOW MAGNETIC FIELDS FORM

In 1820 the Danish scientist Hans Christian Oersted found by accident that the magnetized needle of a compass would realign if brought near a current-carrying wire. The diagram on page 47 shows how the needle would point if placed at various positions in a plane perpendicular to a conductor carrying electrons upward. If the direction of the current were reversed, the compass needle would reverse its orientation.

Apparently a magnetic field encircles the current-carrying wire. This magnetic field can be represented as a series of concentric field lines, which form closed loops, in planes perpendicular to the current. A simple rule allows the prediction of the field direction if the direction of electron motion is known: if the wire is encircled by the fingers of one's left hand, with the thumb pointing in the direction of electron motion, the magnetic field lines encircle the wire in the same direction as the fingers, and a compass needle will align itself tangent to these lines. For a moving positive charge, the right hand is used to predict the magnetic field direction. (The direction of a magnetic field is taken as the direction in which the north-seeking pole of a compass needle points.)

A magnetic field is produced around any moving electric

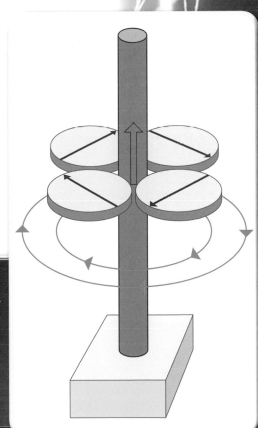

Moving electric charges produce magnetic fields. Magnetic lines of force encircle a conductor (vertical rod) through which electrons are moving. Compass needles placed near the conductor are deflected by the magnetic lines of force.
Encyclopædia Britannica, Inc.

HISTORY OF ELECTRO-MAGNETISM AND ITS APPLICATION TO THE TELEGRAPH.

By Professor Charles A. Joy, Ph. D.

The first fact of electro-magnetism was discovered by Hans Christian Oersted, of Copenhagen, in the Winter of 1819-20. His observation was as follows: If a wire be placed close above or below and parallel to a magnetic needle, and a galvanic current be passed through the wire, the needle will tend to place itself at right angles to it. To the ordinary mind there was very little in this experiment to merit so much fame; and yet, without it no form of the electro-magnetic telegraph were possible; no dynamo-electric machine could be thought of; the electric light would have been vailed in darkness, and the telephone could not have spoken.

It is upon such trifling discoveries as this that the grand edifice of science is founded, and the structure raised which carries civilization forward toward its highest culmination. The truth is, life is made up of trifles, as society is composed of individuals. The sum of many small things makes up a magnificent whole. The added links of apparently unimportant discoveries constitute a chain of inseverable strength.

Ours is an age of small things, and it is also one of progress; because the wise are less confounded by the foolish things of the world than they were in times gone

electricity and magnetism, and, as early as 1812, in his lectures, had dwelt upon the probability that some day this identity would be proved; little thinking that to himself would be due the immortal discovery. During the Winter of 1819-20, Oersted delivered his usual course of lectures on physics, at the University of Copenhagen. While engaged in showing to his pupils the powerful heat which was produced when the connecting wires of a galvanic battery were brought together, he noticed that a magnetic needle which happened to be on the table began to oscillate violently, and to be sensitive to the current passing through the wires. This phenomenon filled him with astonishment, and was immediately made the subject of an exhaustive study, resulting in the discovery and foundation of the great science of electro-magnetism.

Oersted made known his discovery in the month of July, 1820, in a pamphlet of four pages, written in Latin, and entitled: "Experimenta circum effectum conflictus Electrici in Arcum Magneticum" (Experiments on the action of the Electric Current on the Magnetic Needle). This was soon translated into all of the European languages, and attracted great attention. On Monday, September 11, 1820, De la Rive, who had arrived from Geneva, repeated the experiment before the Academy of Sciences, in Paris; and on the following Monday, Ampère announced a second experiment, which supplemented Oersted's and completed the discovery of electro-magnetism.

DISCOVERY OF ELECTRO-MAGNETISM BY OERSTED IN 1820.

Hans Christian Oersted was born on the Danish island

charge, positive or negative, whether in a conductor or in free space. The German-born theoretical physicist Albert Einstein showed in his theory of relativity that the magnetic field produced by a moving electric charge is caused by a warping of the charge's electric field; this is caused by its relative motion. An observer moving along with the charge would not detect any magnetic effects. Thus an electric charge at rest relative to an observer does not produce a magnetic field.

CURRENTS IN A MAGNETIC FIELD

All magnetism arises from moving electric charge. If a current flows in a coil of wire, called a solenoid, the magnetic field will be directed through the solenoid and out one end. The field curves around and reenters the other end of the solenoid. This is similar to the shape of the magnetic field around a bar magnet with a south and north pole, which led the French physicist André-Marie Ampère to speculate in the early 1820s that the magnetic field of a bar magnet is produced by circulating currents in the magnet. Today it is believed that those circulating currents are caused by the motions of electrons, particularly by their spin within individual

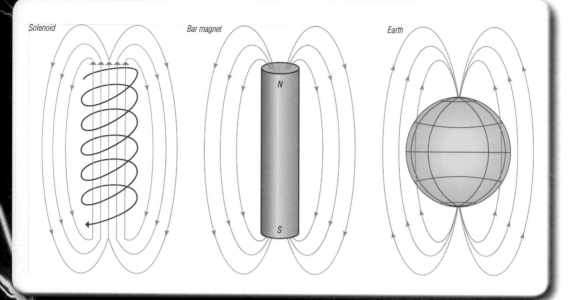

Solenoid   Bar magnet   Earth

The electromagnetism of a current-carrying solenoid, the ferromagnetism of a bar magnet, and the geomagnetism of Earth all produce similar magnetic fields. **Encyclopædia Britannica, Inc.**

atoms. The tiny magnetic fields of the individual atoms align themselves into domains in which the magnetic effects add together. (Physicists are reluctant to picture electrons as actually spinning, however, because quantum theory indicates that it is impossible to prove such motion by experiment.)

If an unmagnetized iron rod is inserted into a solenoid, the magnetic field inside the solenoid forces the electrons in the iron

APPLICATIONS OF MAGNETISM

Magnetic tape recorders and video recorders demonstrate practical uses for the magnetic field produced by an electric current. In tape recording, as current varies in a tape head (itself an electromagnet), the magnetized particles on the tape are realigned to conform to the magnetic field produced by the changing current. Digital video recorders and computer hard drives use magnetically coated disks to record data in a similar way.

In the picture tubes of traditional televisions, magnetic fields are used to steer the electrons from the cathode. As the magnetic field strength is varied, the electrons are deflected so that they scan across the screen. In a loudspeaker, the current from the amplifier is fed to a coil of wire attached to the speaker cone. The coil is arranged so that it is in line with a permanent magnet. As current in the coil is varied, the moving charges are deflected by the field of the permanent magnet. As the coil moves, the cone of the speaker vibrates, causing sound waves to be produced. In addition, powerful magnetic fields keep charged particles moving in circles in the rings of high-energy accelerators used to investigate the substructure of protons and neutrons.

atoms to align their spins, producing domains that reinforce the magnetic field strength. This arrangement of solenoid and iron rod is an electromagnet and gives a magnetic field considerably stronger than that caused by the current in the solenoid alone.

DEFLECTION IN A MAGNETIC FIELD

Moving electric charges are surrounded by a magnetic field, and magnetic fields interact with magnets. Thus it is not surprising that charges moving through a magnetic field experience a deflecting force. What is surprising is the direction of the force. For deflection

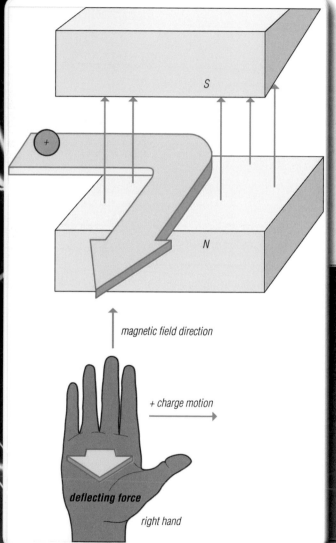

magnetic field direction

+ charge motion

deflecting force

right hand

A positive charge (top) moving perpendicularly through a magnetic field is deflected. The right-hand rule (bottom) predicts the direction in which the positive charge will be deflected. A similar left-hand rule predicts the deflection of negative charges. Encyclopædia Britannica, Inc.

to occur, the charge must have some component of its motion perpendicular to the magnetic field. An electric charge—whether positive or negative—that is moving parallel to the lines of force of the magnetic field will not be acted on by any force from the field. However, a positive charge that moves across the field from left to right will be deflected by an outward force. If the positive charge moves from right to left, it is deflected inward. A negative charge moving across the field will be deflected oppositely.

The deflection for positive charges can be predicted by

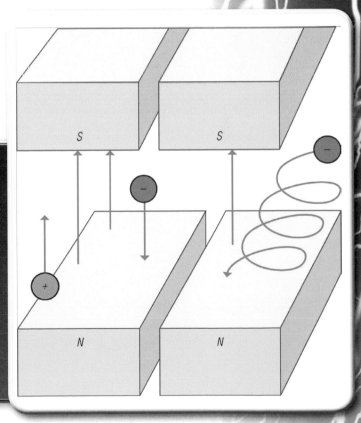

Electric charges (left) that move parallel to magnetic lines of force are not deflected; they continue to move at constant velocity. A charge (right) that moves neither parallel nor perpendicular to the field spirals through the field. Encyclopædia Britannica, Inc.

positioning the right hand so that the thumb points in the direction of the moving positive charge and the fingers point in the direction of the magnetic field. (Magnetic fields point away from north poles and toward south poles.) The positive charge will be deflected from its original path in a direction out of the palm of the hand. A similar left-hand rule applies to negative charges moving across magnetic fields.

CHAPTER 5

MOTORS AND GENERATORS

The interaction between moving charges and a magnetic field makes possible two very useful devices: the electric motor and the generator. In a motor, electrical energy is converted into energy of motion. In a generator, the reverse process takes place: mechanical energy is converted into electrical energy.

MOTORS

A simple motor can be represented as a loop of wire attached to a source of direct current (DC). The loop is pivoted to rotate in a magnetic field. As electric charge moves along the loop, magnetic forces deflect the charge, causing the loop to rotate. To keep the loop rotating, the direction of current in the loop must be reversed every 180 degrees. A device called a split-ring commutator is used for this purpose.

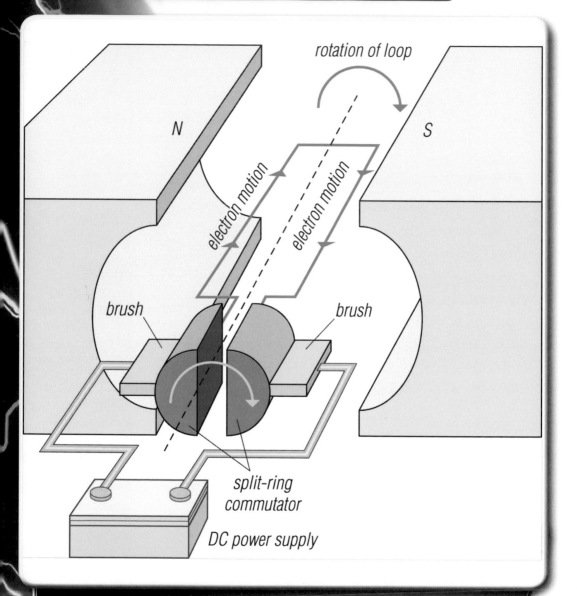

rotation of loop

N

S

electron motion

electron motion

brush

brush

split-ring
commutator

DC power supply

In a DC motor, electrons from the DC power supply cause the wire loop to rotate in a clockwise direction, converting electrical energy into mechanical energy. **Encyclopædia Britannica, Inc.**

Another design is the induction motor, in which a magnetic field revolves around a piece of metal and creates eddy currents in the metal. These currents produce magnetic fields that interact with the revolving field. This makes the metal rotate if it is pivoted properly. The rotating metal constitutes a motor. The smallest motors of this type use a rotor (revolving part) made of metal disks notched at the edges to place the eddy currents properly. Larger types may use a squirrel-cage rotor. This is made of metal bars arranged to form a skeleton cylinder. The ends of the bars may be attached to disks, or the bars may be mounted on a cylinder of enameled iron and connected at the ends. The eddy currents flow through the bars and end connections.

The revolving fields are produced by using two-phase or three-phase current to energize the field coils. The phases amount to different alternating currents (AC) in the same circuit. Because different-phase currents can be used, induction motors are classified as polyphase. The currents reach maximum and minimum strengths in each direction of flow at different times. The field coils are connected to place

maximums at different points in turn around a circle. This produces the revolving field.

Synchronous motors use a polyphase current to provide revolving fields in the stator (stationary part), and other current (sometimes direct) gives the rotor a field that follows the stator fields around. Such motors run at constant speeds, proportional to the frequency of the supplied current.

GENERATORS

A generator is a motor working in reverse: a motor changes electrical energy into mechanical energy, but a generator produces electrical energy *from* mechanical energy. Superficially the diagram of a generator appears identical to that of a motor. Each consists of a loop of wire that can rotate in a magnetic field. In a motor, electric current is fed into the loop, resulting in rotation of the loop. In the generator, the loop is rotated, resulting in the production of electric current in the loop. For 180 degrees of the rotation, electron deflection produces an electric current in the loop that moves in one direction; for the next 180

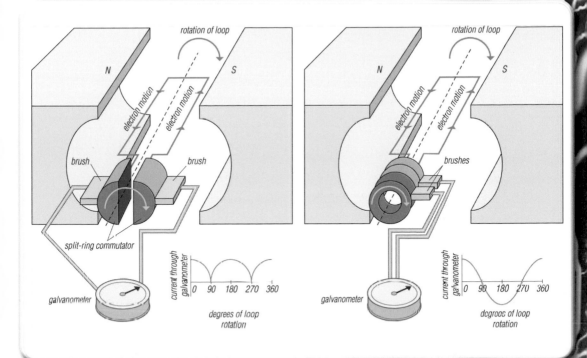

*Electric current in the loop of a DC generator (left) alternates— that is, it changes directions—but in the outer circuit it travels in only one direction and drops to zero twice with each rotation of the loop. By arranging more loops, a steadier direct current can be obtained. In an AC generator (right) the current is alternating in both the loop and in the outer circuit. **Encyclopædia Britannica, Inc.***

degrees, the electron deflection is reversed. As the current leaves the loop to an external circuit, it moves in one direction and then the other. This is alternating current.

PRODUCING ELECTRICITY

Generators do not create energy. To produce electricity either the loop or the magnets must be rotated relative to one another. The energy for this rotation can be provided by a variety of sources. In some sources water is converted to steam, which is used to drive turbines that operate generators. The energy to boil the water and convert it to steam comes from burning coal, oil, or natural gas, or from the heat released by controlled nuclear reactions. The rotation may be driven by the gravitational potential energy stored in water held behind the dam of a hydroelectric plant, by wind in wind turbines, or by the steam produced naturally within Earth.

Some notable sources of power include (clockwise from top, opposite page) *wind, coal, falling water, and the splitting of atoms, which releases nuclear energy.* Bloomberg via Getty Images, Saul Loeb/AFP/Getty Images, John Nordell/Christian Science Monitor/Getty Images, Bloomberg via Getty Images

For a generator to generate direct current it is necessary to use a split-ring commutator at the point where the generator feeds current to the external circuit. The current in the loop is still alternating, but it is direct in the external circuit.

ELECTROMAGNETIC INDUCTION

The scientists Michael Faraday of England and Joseph Henry of the United States independently showed in 1831 that moving a magnet through a coil of wire would generate a current in the wire. If the magnet was plunged into the coil, current flowed one way. When the magnet was removed, the current direction was reversed. This phenomenon is called electromagnetic induction, and it is the principle underlying the operation of the generator. As long as the magnet and the coil move relative to each other, a potential difference is produced across the coil, and current flows in the coil. A potential difference is also produced if the magnetic field through the coil grows stronger or weaker. The greater the rate at which the magnetic field changes, the greater the potential difference produced.

The key is that the magnetic field must be changing.

In 1864 the Scottish physicist James Clerk Maxwell suggested: (1) If an electric field changes with time, a magnetic field is induced at right angles to the changing electric field. The greater the rate at which the electric field changes, the stronger the induced magnetic field. (2) If a magnetic field changes with time, an electric field is induced at right angles to the changing magnetic field. The greater the rate at which the magnetic field changes, the stronger the induced electric field.

Maxwell calculated that these electric and magnetic fields would propagate each other and travel through space as time-varying fields. The speed of these electromagnetic waves is 3.0×10^8 (300,000,000) meters per second. That happens to be the same as the speed of light. In fact, visible light is merely a narrow range of frequencies in what is known as the electromagnetic spectrum. As people read a printed page, electromagnetic waves reflected from the page pass into their eyes. As the electric field of that wave reaches the eye's retina, electrons in molecules of the retina interact with the

James Clerk Maxwell, c. 1860s. On the next page is the most complete formulation of his theory on electromagnetism, A Treatise on Electricity and Magnetism, *which he published in 1873.* SSPL via Getty Images

field, change position, and start the message to the brain that eventually allows a person to understand what has been read.

LENZ'S LAW

Whenever a changing magnetic field generates a current in a coil of wire, the current will generate its own magnetic field. That induced magnetic field will always tend to oppose the change in the magnetic field that induced it. This rule was first suggested by the Russian-born physicist Heinrich F.E. Lenz in 1834. The effects of the induced field can be observed during the operation of a hand-cranked generator. When the generator is cranked slowly,

Clarendon Press Series

A TREATISE

ON

ELECTRICITY AND MAGNETISM

BY

JAMES CLERK MAXWELL, M.A.

LLD. EDIN., F.R.SS. LONDON AND EDINBURGH
HONORARY FELLOW OF TRINITY COLLEGE,
AND PROFESSOR OF EXPERIMENTAL PHYSICS
IN THE UNIVERSITY OF CAMBRIDGE

VOL. I

Oxford
AT THE CLARENDON PRESS
1873

[All rights reserved]

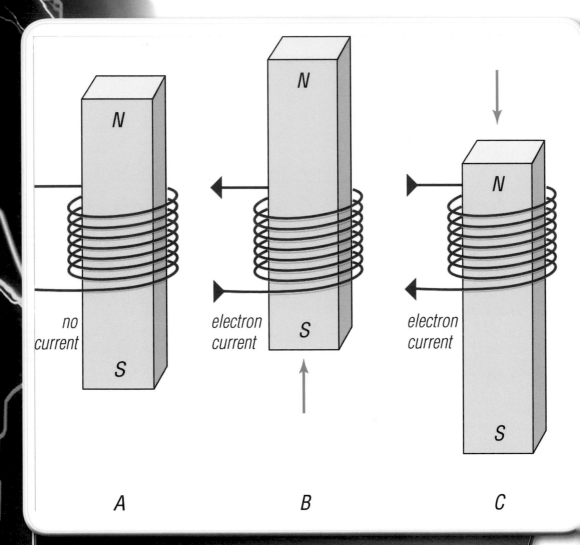

No electric current is induced when magnet A is at rest with respect to the loop. When magnet B is pushed up through the loop, a current is induced. When magnet C is dropped through the loop, current is induced in the opposite direction. Encyclopædia Britannica, Inc.

little current is produced and weak electro-magnetic forces oppose the rotation. But as the cranking rate is increased and more current is produced, the forces on the rotating loop become stronger, and the loop is correspondingly more difficult to turn.

Lenz's law also applies to motors, where a current-carrying wire moves in a magnetic field. That movement, in turn, produces a current in the wire that opposes the original direction of current in the wire. Because electric current cannot occur without a potential difference, this opposition effect is sometimes called a back-emf. When a motor is started, a large current flows at first, and, as the motor begins to turn rapidly, a large back-emf is induced and the net current in the motor drops. If a large load is suddenly added to the motor, slowing it drastically, the back-emf will drop, and the sudden rise in current may cause overheating and burn out the motor.

Even a simple coil of wire in a DC circuit exhibits the effects of back-emf. As the current in the coil increases, the changing magnetic field produced around the coil will tend to produce a back-emf. This is called self-inductance. Normally the current in a

circuit rises rapidly after the switch is closed. But in this circuit, the current rises relatively slowly. On the other hand, when the switch is opened, the current in the circuit normally falls to zero almost instantly. But as the magnetic field around the coil decreases, an emf is generated that tends to keep the current from decaying as rapidly. A coil like this is used in devices designed to prevent damage to electronic equipment caused by voltage spikes—sudden increases in potential difference that would tend to produce rapidly changing currents.

Conclusion

Electricity is a fundamental and ever-present form of energy. As such, it has been a subject of interest among scientists since ancient times. The earliest recorded observations about electricity date from about 600 BC, when the Greek philosopher Thales of Miletus noted that when amber, a fossil resin, was rubbed it would attract feathers or bits of straw. Thales was the first in a long line of individuals who gradually uncovered the mysteries of this force, illuminating the nature of electric charges, currents, and circuits.

Just as important are the practical inventors who have applied the principles of electricity in a wide variety of devices. Two of the most famous were Thomas Edison and Alexander Graham Bell, who introduced the electric lightbulb and the telephone, respectively, in the late 1800s. The continuous stream of electronic innovations that followed—from appliances to radio and television to computers—has revolutionized daily life. Without electricity, the interconnected world that we take for granted in the 21st century would be inconceivable.

absolute zero In physics, the temperature at which molecular movement virtually stops and there is a complete absence of heat (−273.15° on the Celsius scale, −459.67° on the Fahrenheit scale).

ampere A unit of electric current named after French physicist André-Marie Ampère. One ampere is equivalent to a flow of one coulomb per second or to the steady current produced by one volt applied across a resistance of one ohm.

cathode Negative terminal or electrode at which electrons enter a system, such as an electrolytic cell or an electron tube.

coulomb A unit of electric charge named after French physicist Charles-Augustin de Coulomb. A coulomb is the quantity of electricity transported by a current of one ampere in one second.

eddy current Motion of electric charge induced within a metal by a changing electric or magnetic field or by electro-magnetic waves.

electrode An electric conductor that acts as a current pathway into and out of a medium (such as a storage battery).

electron A negatively charged particle located outside the atomic nucleus, an

electron is the lightest stable subatomic particle known.

ferromagnetism A physical phenomenon in which certain electrically uncharged materials, such as iron, strongly attract others.

fluorescent Capable of absorbing and then quickly reemitting electromagnetic radiation.

geomagnetism Terrestrial magnetism; Earth's magnetic field.

ion An atom that has one or more positive or negative electrical charges.

joule Named after English physicist James Joule, a joule is a unit used for measuring energy or work done.

kinetic energy The energy of an object in motion. All moving objects—including atoms—have kinetic energy.

newton A unit for measuring force, the newton is named after English physicist and mathematician Sir Isaac Newton.

ohm Named after German physicist Georg Simon Ohm, an ohm is a unit for measuring how much electrical resistance a substance gives to the flow of a current running through it.

polyphase Having or producing two or more phases.

proton Located in the nucleus of an atom, a proton is a tiny particle that carries a positive electrical charge.

solenoid A coil of wire, usually in cylindrical form, that when carrying a current acts like a magnet.

split-ring commutator A device within a motor that keeps it rotating by reversing the direction of the electric current every half turn.

tangent Touching but not intersecting.

vector Shown by arrows, vectors represent quantities that have both a specific magnitude—size or strength—and direction. Velocity, for example, has both magnitude and direction.

American Institute of Physics (AIP)
One Physics Ellipse
College Park, MD 20740
(301) 209-3100
Web site: http://www.aip.org
The members of the AIP are professionals,
    academics, and educators who seek to
    promote the study of physics among the
    public through programs, publications,
    and outreach services.

The Bakken Museum
3537 Zenith Avenue South
Minneapolis, MN 55416
(612) 926-3878
Web site: http://www.thebakken.org
With unique exhibits highlighting the
    history and nature of electricity and
    magnetism, as well as exciting school and
    youth programs, the Bakken Museum
    inspires public interest in the sciences.
    Many of the volumes in its extensive
    library chronicle the history of electric-
    ity and magnetism and are available to
    the public.

Canadian Association of Physicists (CAP)
Suite 112, MacDonald Building
University of Ottawa

150 Louis Pasteur Priv.
Ottawa, ON K1N 6N5
Canada
(613) 562-5614
Web site: http://www.cap.ca
Committed to advancing research and
education in the field of physics,
CAP provides a number of programs
and resources for professionals in
physics-related careers, lectures and
competitions for students, and informa-
tion and events for the public at large.

Electric Power Research Institute (EPRI)
3420 Hillview Avenue
Palo Alto, CA 94304
(650) 855-2000
Web site: http://my.epri.com
Through its research and development ini-
tiatives, the EPRI aims to improve the
generation, distribution, and use of electricity. Some of its many projects include
supporting emerging technologies to
address the reliability, efficiency, and safety
of electricity.

Science World at TELUS World of Science
1455 Quebec Street
Vancouver, BC V6A 3Z7

Canada
(604) 443-7443
Web site: http://www.scienceworld.ca/
electricity
With interactive exhibits and educational
programs in a variety of subject areas,
including an extensive exhibit on electricity, Science World encourages the
pursuit and enjoyment of scientific
exploration among the public.

WEB SITES

Due to the changing nature of Internet links,
Rosen Educational Services has developed an
online list of Web sites related to the subject
of this book. This site is updated regularly.
Please use this link to access the list:

www.rosenlinks.com/inphy/eletr

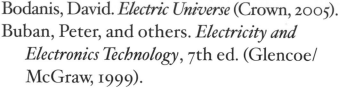
Bodanis, David. *Electric Universe* (Crown, 2005).

Buban, Peter, and others. *Electricity and Electronics Technology*, 7th ed. (Glencoe/McGraw, 1999).

Dreier, David. *Electrical Circuits: Harnessing Electricity* (Compass Point, 2008).

Gibilsco, Stan. *Electricity Demystified* (McGraw, 2005).

Kirkland, Kyle. *Electricity and Magnetism* (Facts On File, 2007).

Panofsky, W.K. and Phillips, Melba. *Classical Electricity and Magnetism*, 2nd ed. (Dover, 2005).

Parker, Steve. *Electricity*, rev. ed. (DK, 2005).

Parker, Steve. *Fully Charged: Electricity* (Heinemann, 2005).

Solway, Andrew. *Generating and Using Electricity* (Heinemann, 2009).

Tucker, Tom. *Bolt of Fate: Benjamin Franklin and the Electric Kite Hoax* (Public Affairs, 2003).